Knowledge MASTERS

JUNIOR ATLAS

Contents

Written and designed by
ony Potter • Nicola Wright •
hristine Wilson • Dee Turner

Illustrated by
Lyn Mitchell

N E
W S

zigzag

All about maps

A map is a picture of a place seen from above. Imagine what your home would look like if you flew over it in an aeroplane and took a photograph. The picture would show the area around your home spread out flat.

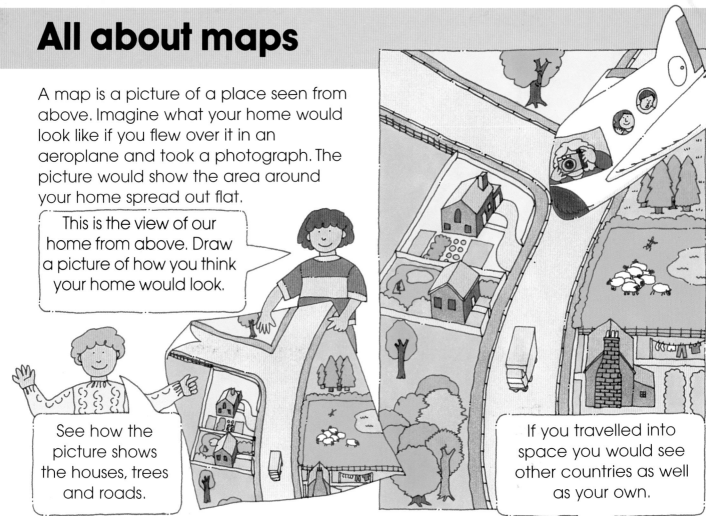

This is the view of our home from above. Draw a picture of how you think your home would look.

See how the picture shows the houses, trees and roads.

If you travelled into space you would see other countries as well as your own.

My town

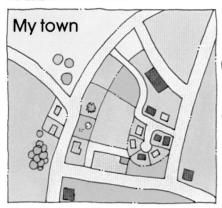

Imagine that you fly higher. Now you can see your whole town or city. Everything looks tiny.

My country

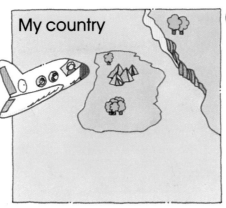

Imagine your town is on an island. As you go even higher you can see the whole island.

The Earth

Clouds form in the sky and swirl around the Earth. There is much more ocean than land.

This is how my country would look as a map. Tiny pictures called symbols are used to stand for real things.

2

The pictures below are the symbols used in this book. This part of an atlas is called the **key**. The key tells you what the symbols stand for.

If you are looking for a country, go to the list on page 32 and look under the first letter of the country name.
So, **Chile** is under the letter **C**.

Symbols

 **Country boundaries**

 **Oceans and Seas**

 **Capital cities**   ■ Moscow

Large cities   ● Vladivostok

 **Lakes**

Rivers

 **High mountains**

Low mountains

 **Tropical rain forest**

 **Monsoon woodland** (hot areas with a rainy season)

 **Pine forest**

Symbols

 **Leafy woodland**

Mixed woodland

Mediterranean woodland (dry areas with evergreen trees)

Desert (some deserts are just sandy, but some are stony and covered with bushes or cacti)

Grassland (called **prairie** in North America, and **pampas** in South America)

 **Steppe** (scrubland or grassland in Asia)

 **Savannah** (dry grasslands with some trees in Africa)

 **Tundra** (frozen land)

 **Ice**

3

World map

This big map shows you what the world would look like if it were flattened out. The differently coloured areas of land are called continents. There are seven continents and four oceans.

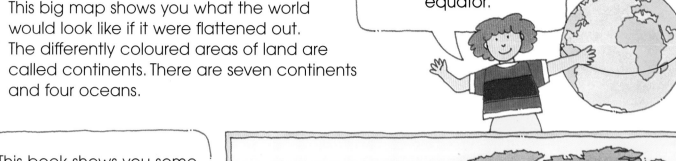

This is planet Earth. Imagine a line around its middle. This is called the equator.

This book shows you some of the people, animals, plants and places found in each continent.

The biggest continent is Asia. The smallest continent is Australia.

Countries

The maps in this book show all the countries in the world. A white line shows where one country joins another.

Every country has a flag. Some of them are shown in this book.

The Polish flag

The Belgian flag

The Portuguese flag

The Italian flag

The bottom half of the world is called the southern hemisphere.

North America

Arctic Ocean

Atlantic Ocean

Equator

Pacific Ocean

South America

Atlantic Ocean

South Pole

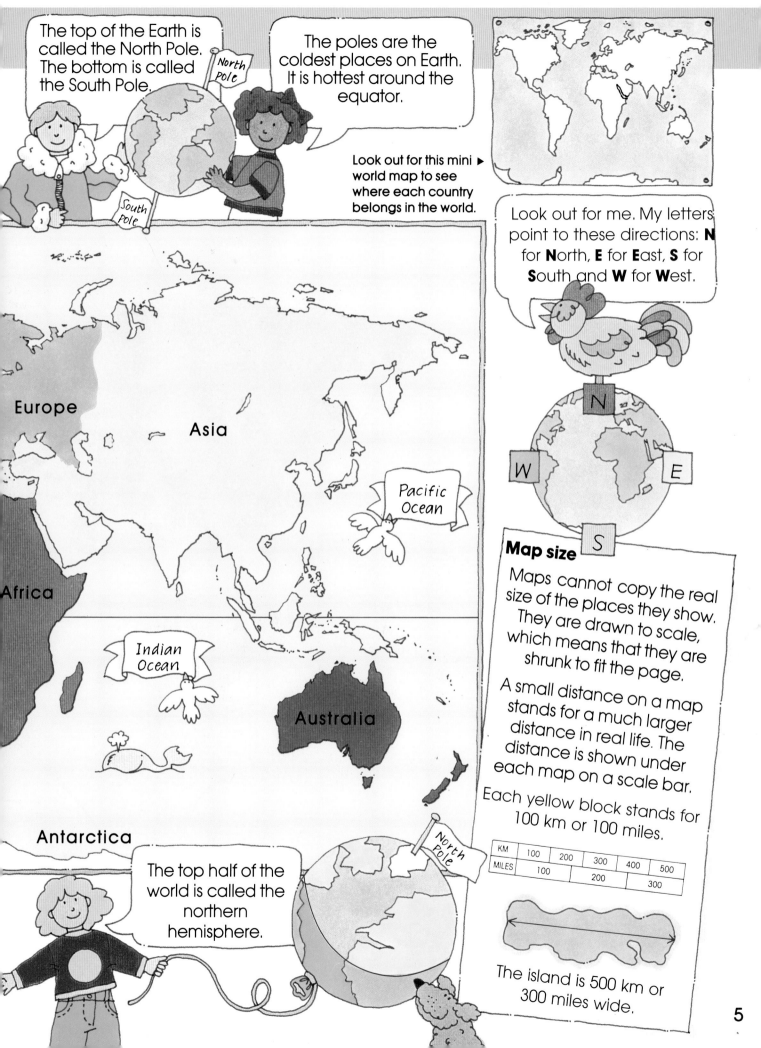

The top of the Earth is called the North Pole. The bottom is called the South Pole.

North Pole

South Pole

The poles are the coldest places on Earth. It is hottest around the equator.

Look out for this mini ▶ world map to see where each country belongs in the world.

Look out for me. My letters point to these directions: **N** for **N**orth, **E** for **E**ast, **S** for **S**outh and **W** for **W**est.

N

W   E

S

Europe

Asia

Pacific Ocean

Africa

Indian Ocean

Australia

Antarctica

The top half of the world is called the northern hemisphere.

North Pole

Map size

Maps cannot copy the real size of the places they show. They are drawn to scale, which means that they are shrunk to fit the page.

A small distance on a map stands for a much larger distance in real life. The distance is shown under each map on a scale bar.

Each yellow block stands for 100 km or 100 miles.

KM	100	200	300	400	500
MILES	100		200		300

The island is 500 km or 300 miles wide.

5

North America

INTERNET LINK http://www.geography.state.gov/htmls/plugin.html
Find out about the exciting places in the world where US diplomats live.

North America contains Canada, the United States of America, Mexico, the countries of Central America and the West Indies. Canada is the second largest country in the world. The USA is the fourth largest and has fifty states.

The Canadian flag

Ice hockey is a very popular sport in Canada.

Skiing is popular in the Rocky Mountains. The Rockies run from Canada through the USA.

The USA produces more timber than any other country.

Some Canadian police are called Mounties. Some still ride horses, but most drive cars or motorcycles nowadays.

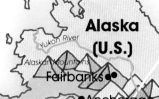

Alaska (U.S.)
Yukon River
Alaskan Mountains
Fairbanks
Anchorage
Great Bear Lake
Mackenzie River
Great Slave Lake
Lake Athabasca
Rocky Mountains
Columbia River
Snake River
Coastal Mountains
Sierra Nevada
Colorado River

Vancouver

Fact file

Highest mountain: Mount McKinley, Alaska, 6,194 m (20,322 ft).

Longest river: Mississippi River, USA, 3,779 km (2,384 miles).

Largest lake: Lake Superior, 82,103 sq km (31,700 sq miles).

Weather: Canada and Alaska are the coldest parts of North America. It is hot in central America and the West Indies.

Biggest city: New York, USA, about 7 million people.

Number of people: Canada, about 31 million. USA, about 273 million. Mexico, about 100 million. Costa Rica, about 3.7 million. Panama, about 2.8 million.

One of the world's most active volcanos, Mauna Loa, is on the island of Hawaii.

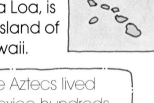
Hawaii (USA)

Los Angeles
San Diego

The American flag

Pacific Ocean

The Aztecs lived in Mexico hundreds of years ago. Mexicans are proud of their Aztec ancestry.

Bananas, coffee and sugar are grown in Central America.

The Mexican flag

6

KM	250	500	1000	1500	2000	2500	3000	3500	4000	4500	5000	5500	6000	6500
MILES		250	500	1000		1500		2000		2500		3000	3500		4000

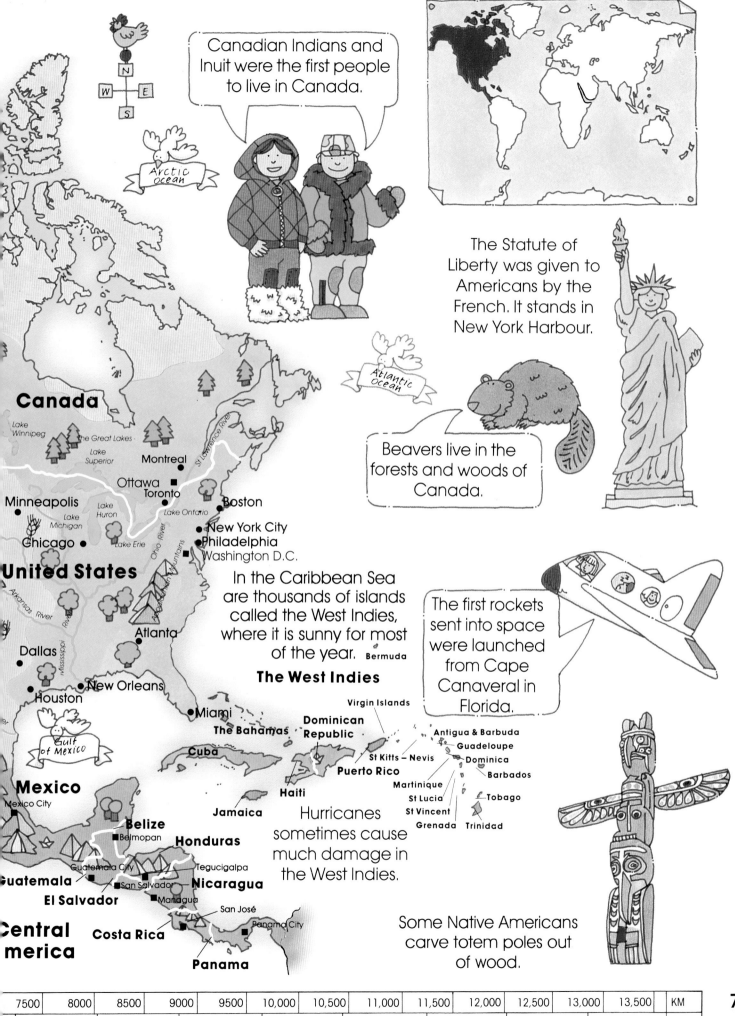

South America

South America is the fourth largest continent. It is made up of 13 different countries. There are mountains and rain forests as well as plains and deserts. The weather ranges from very hot to very cold.

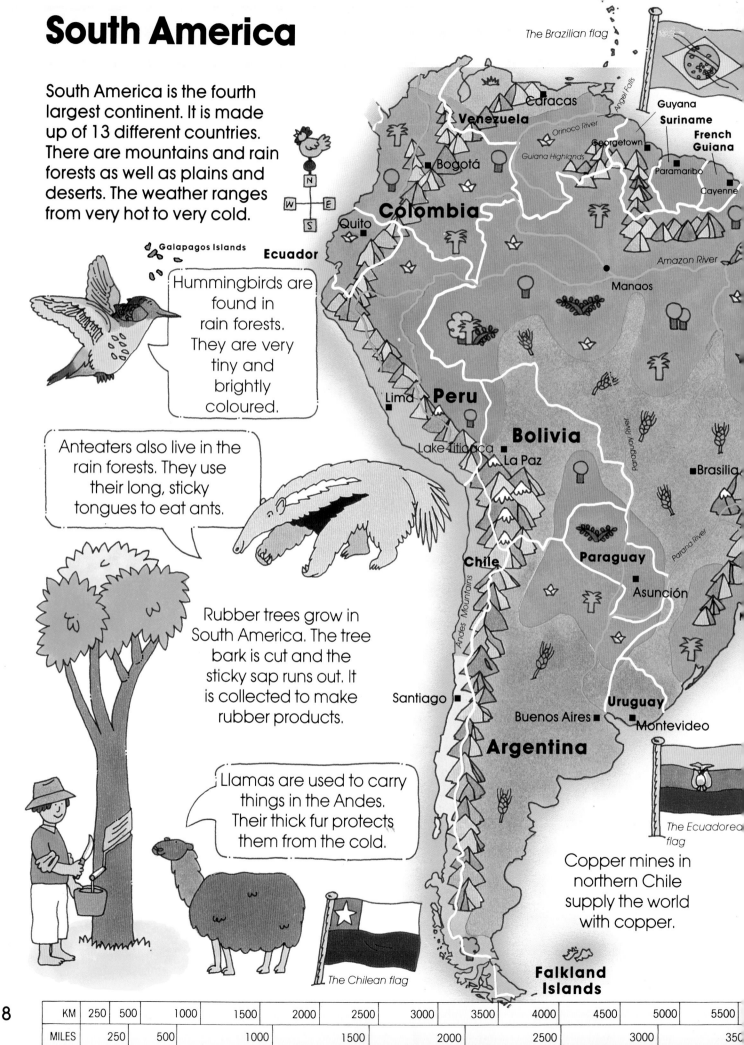

The Brazilian flag

Galapagos Islands

Hummingbirds are found in rain forests. They are very tiny and brightly coloured.

Anteaters also live in the rain forests. They use their long, sticky tongues to eat ants.

Rubber trees grow in South America. The tree bark is cut and the sticky sap runs out. It is collected to make rubber products.

Llamas are used to carry things in the Andes. Their thick fur protects them from the cold.

Copper mines in northern Chile supply the world with copper.

The Ecuadorean flag

The Chilean flag

Caracas
Venezuela
Guyana
Suriname
French Guiana
Orinoco River
Angel Falls
Georgetown
Bogotá
Guiana Highlands
Paramaribo
Colombia
Cayenne
Quito
Ecuador
Amazon River
Manaos
Peru
Lima
Bolivia
Lake Titicaca
La Paz
Brasilia
Paraguay River
Paraguay
Asunción
Parana River
Chile
Andes Mountains
Santiago
Uruguay
Buenos Aires
Montevideo
Argentina
Falkland Islands

KM	250	500	1000	1500	2000	2500	3000	3500	4000	4500	5000	5500
MILES		250	500	1000		1500		2000		2500		3000	350

8

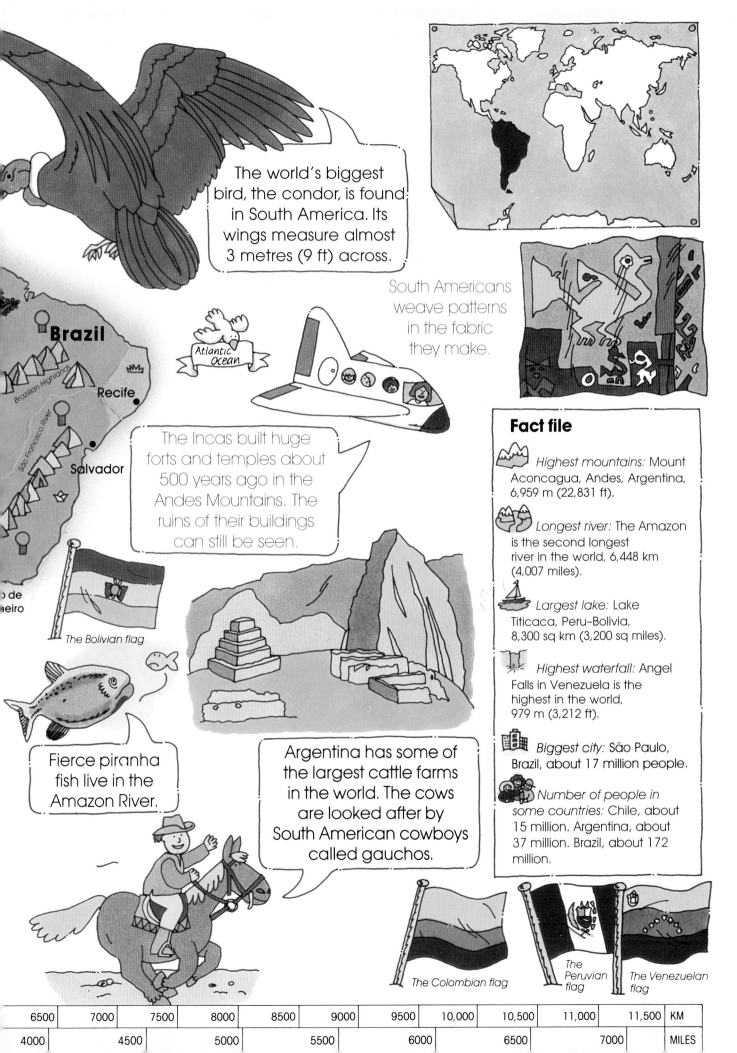

The world's biggest bird, the condor, is found in South America. Its wings measure almost 3 metres (9 ft) across.

South Americans weave patterns in the fabric they make.

Brazil

Brazilian Highlands

Recife

São Francisco River

Salvador

o de eiro

Atlantic ocean

The Incas built huge forts and temples about 500 years ago in the Andes Mountains. The ruins of their buildings can still be seen.

The Bolivian flag

Fierce piranha fish live in the Amazon River.

Argentina has some of the largest cattle farms in the world. The cows are looked after by South American cowboys called gauchos.

Fact file

Highest mountains: Mount Aconcagua, Andes, Argentina, 6,959 m (22,831 ft).

Longest river: The Amazon is the second longest river in the world, 6,448 km (4,007 miles).

Largest lake: Lake Titicaca, Peru–Bolivia, 8,300 sq km (3,200 sq miles).

Highest waterfall: Angel Falls in Venezuela is the highest in the world, 979 m (3,212 ft).

Biggest city: São Paulo, Brazil, about 17 million people.

Number of people in some countries: Chile, about 15 million. Argentina, about 37 million. Brazil, about 172 million.

The Colombian flag

The Peruvian flag

The Venezuelan flag

6500	7000	7500	8000	8500	9000	9500	10,000	10,500	11,000	11,500	KM
4000		4500		5000		5500		6000		6500		7000		MILES

Northern Europe

The northern European countries are known as Scandinavia. Norway has over 150,000 islands along its coastline. The Norwegian coast is jagged, with deep inlets called fjords. Forests and lakes cover large areas of Scandinavia. Many bears and wolves used to live in the forests.

Workers travel to the oil rigs by helicopter.

Children here learn to ski almost as soon as they can walk!

There is oil under the sea bed. Oil rigs are used to pump the oil up to the surface.

Norwegian Sea

The oil is used as fuel for cars and for heating buildings.

North Sea

Trawlers are fishing boats that catch fish by dragging nets along the sea bed. Many Norwegian fishing boats fish in the North Sea.

Some fishing boats can stay out at sea for months at a time.

The Danish flag

The Norwegian flag

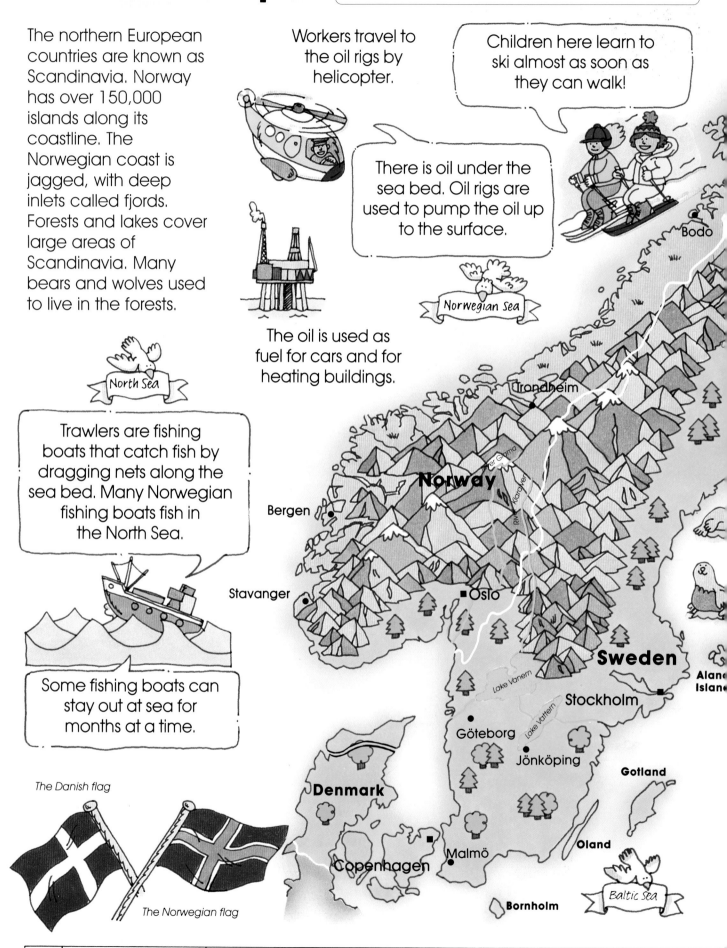

Bodo

Trondheim

River Glåma

Norway

River Klarälven

Bergen

Oslo

Stavanger

Sweden

Lake Vänern

Stockholm

Alan Islan

Göteborg

Lake Vättern

Jönköping

Gotland

Denmark

Oland

Malmö

Copenhagen

Bornholm

Baltic Sea

KM	250	500	1000
MILES	250	500	

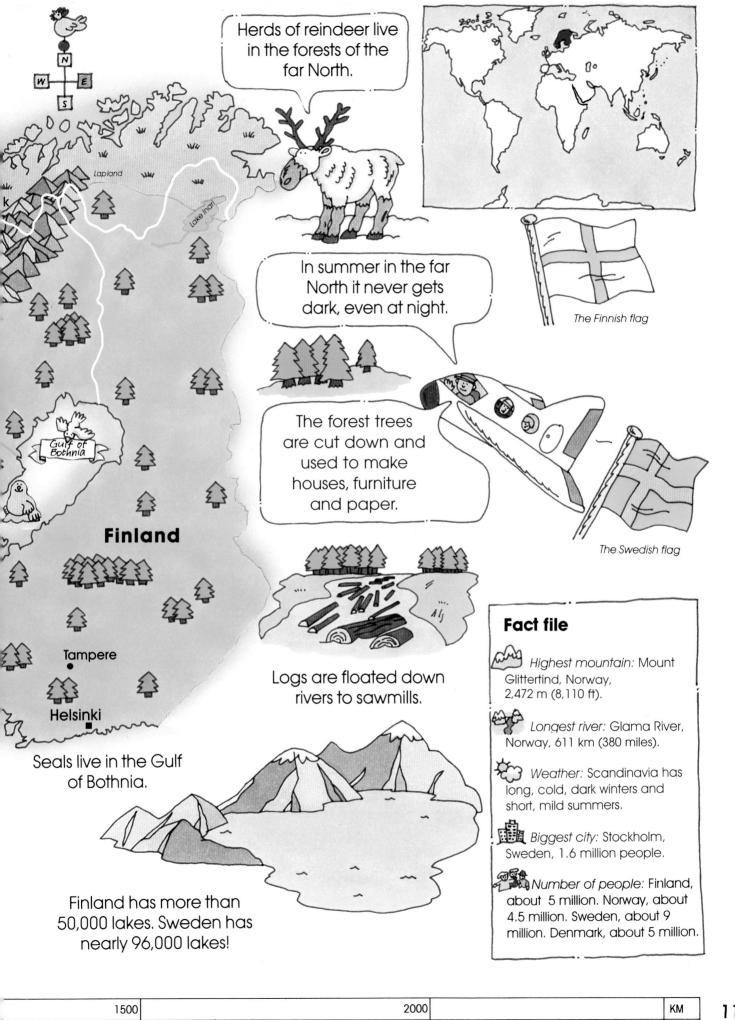

Herds of reindeer live in the forests of the far North.

In summer in the far North it never gets dark, even at night.

The forest trees are cut down and used to make houses, furniture and paper.

The Finnish flag

The Swedish flag

Lapland

Lake Inari

Gulf of Bothnia

Finland

Tampere

Helsinki

Logs are floated down rivers to sawmills.

Seals live in the Gulf of Bothnia.

Finland has more than 50,000 lakes. Sweden has nearly 96,000 lakes!

Fact file

Highest mountain: Mount Glittertind, Norway, 2,472 m (8,110 ft).

Longest river: Glama River, Norway, 611 km (380 miles).

Weather: Scandinavia has long, cold, dark winters and short, mild summers.

Biggest city: Stockholm, Sweden, 1.6 million people.

Number of people: Finland, about 5 million. Norway, about 4.5 million. Sweden, about 9 million. Denmark, about 5 million.

| 1500 | 2000 | KM |
| 1000 | | MILES |

Britain and Central Europe

On this map you can see sixteen different countries. Some, like Luxembourg, are tiny. Others, such as France, are large. There are very high mountains, called the Alps, in Switzerland and Austria, but most of the rest of Europe is flat land. This is very good for farming.

Northern Ireland

Ireland is known as the Emerald Isle because of its beautiful green hills and fields.

Britain used to be joined to the rest of Europe. It became an island a long time ago when sea levels rose.

The British Crown Jewels are kept safely locked up in the Tower of London.

More than 300 different kinds of cheese are made in France.

Grapes are grown in France, Germany and other countries. They are used to make wine.

The Eiffel Tower is in Paris, the capital of France.

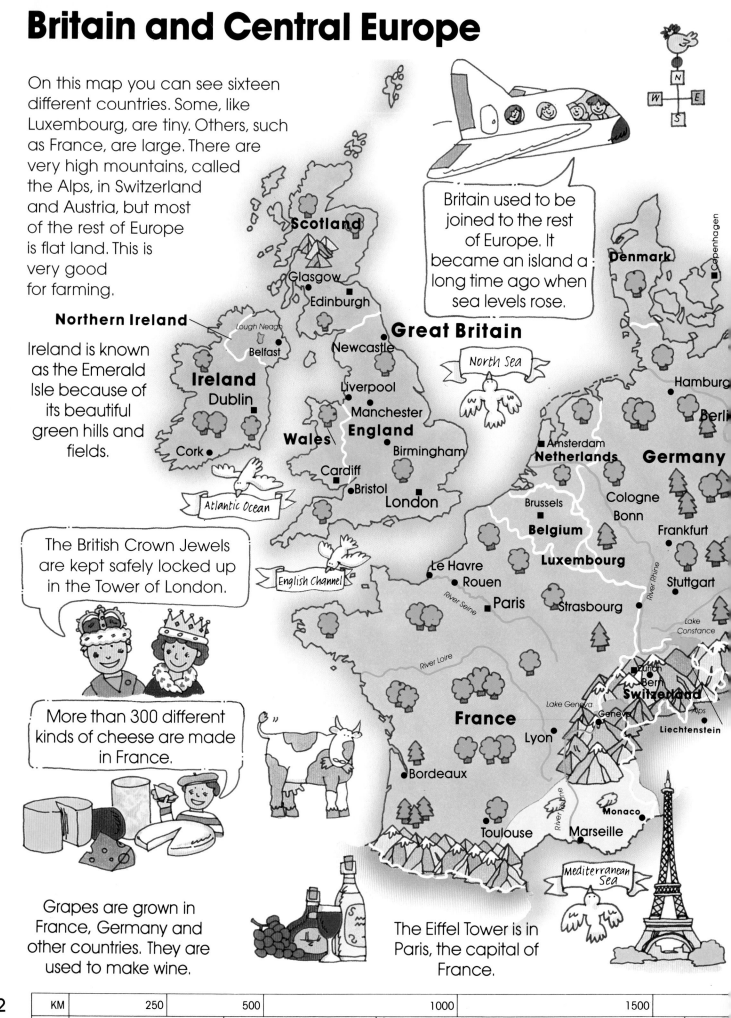

Scotland
Glasgow
Edinburgh
Lough Neagh
Belfast
Great Britain
Newcastle
Ireland
Dublin
Liverpool
Manchester
North Sea
Wales
England
Cork
Birmingham
Cardiff
Bristol
London
Atlantic Ocean
English Channel
Le Havre
Rouen
River Seine
Paris
Brussels
Belgium
Luxembourg
Strasbourg
Amsterdam
Netherlands
Germany
Cologne
Bonn
Frankfurt
Stuttgart
River Rhine
Lake Constance
Denmark
Copenhagen
Hamburg
Berlin
River Loire
France
Lyon
Bordeaux
Zürich
Bern
Switzerland
Lake Geneva
Geneva
Alps
Liechtenstein
Toulouse
River Rhône
Monaco
Marseille
Mediterranean Sea
N E S W

KM		250		500		1000		1500	
MILES			250		500			1000	

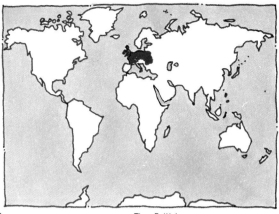

The Netherlands is so flat that the sea can cause floods. Sea walls protect the land, and windmills pump water away. Many Dutch farmers grow flowers.

Gdansk
River Vistula
■Warsaw
•Poznan
Poland
River Oder
Wroclaw
River Elbe
Krakow•
Carpathians
ue
Czech Republic **Slovakia**
Vienna ■
Bratislava ■
■Budapest
Selzburg
Hungary
River Danube
Austria

Germany, France and Britain have big factories making many things from cars to computers.

The Swiss flag
The British Union Jack
The French flag

The German flag
The Austrian flag

Cluj-Napoca
Romania
Constanta
Timisoara
Bucharest■

Bulgaria
Sofia

Fact file

Highest mountain: Mont Blanc, France, 4,807 m (15,771 ft).

Longest river: The Danube, 2,824 km (1,755 miles).

Weather: Most of this part of Europe has mild winters and cool summers. Rain falls all year round. Snow falls on high land in winter.

Biggest city: Paris, France, about 9.6 million people.

Number of people in some European countries: France, about 59 million. United Kingdom (England, Scotland, Wales and Northern Ireland), about 59 million. Germany, about 82 million. Netherlands, about 16 million.

Skiing is a popular sport in the mountains.

There are many fairy-tale castles built along the banks of the Rhine River in Germany.

2000		2500		3000		3500	KM
	1500				2000		MILES

Mediterranean Europe

The countries around the Mediterranean Sea are sunny all year. Olives, fruit and vegetables are grown in all these countries. Many people go to the Mediterranean for vacations. In parts of Spain and Italy there are high mountains where people ski in the winter.

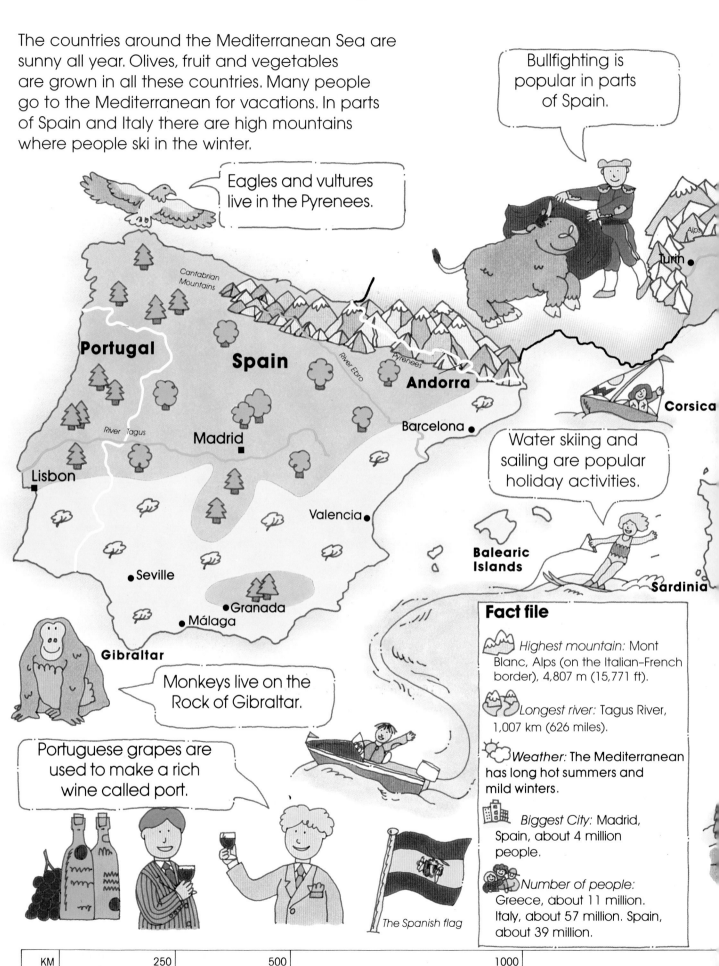

Bullfighting is popular in parts of Spain.

Eagles and vultures live in the Pyrenees.

Water skiing and sailing are popular holiday activities.

Monkeys live on the Rock of Gibraltar.

Portuguese grapes are used to make a rich wine called port.

Cantabrian Mountains

Portugal

Spain

River Ebro

Pyrenees

Andorra

Barcelona

Corsica

River Tagus

Madrid

Lisbon

Valencia

Balearic Islands

Sardinia

Seville

Granada

Málaga

Gibraltar

Turin

Alps

The Spanish flag

Fact file

Highest mountain: Mont Blanc, Alps (on the Italian–French border), 4,807 m (15,771 ft).

Longest river: Tagus River, 1,007 km (626 miles).

Weather: The Mediterranean has long hot summers and mild winters.

Biggest City: Madrid, Spain, about 4 million people.

Number of people: Greece, about 11 million. Italy, about 57 million. Spain, about 39 million.

	KM	250	500	1000
	MILES	250	500	

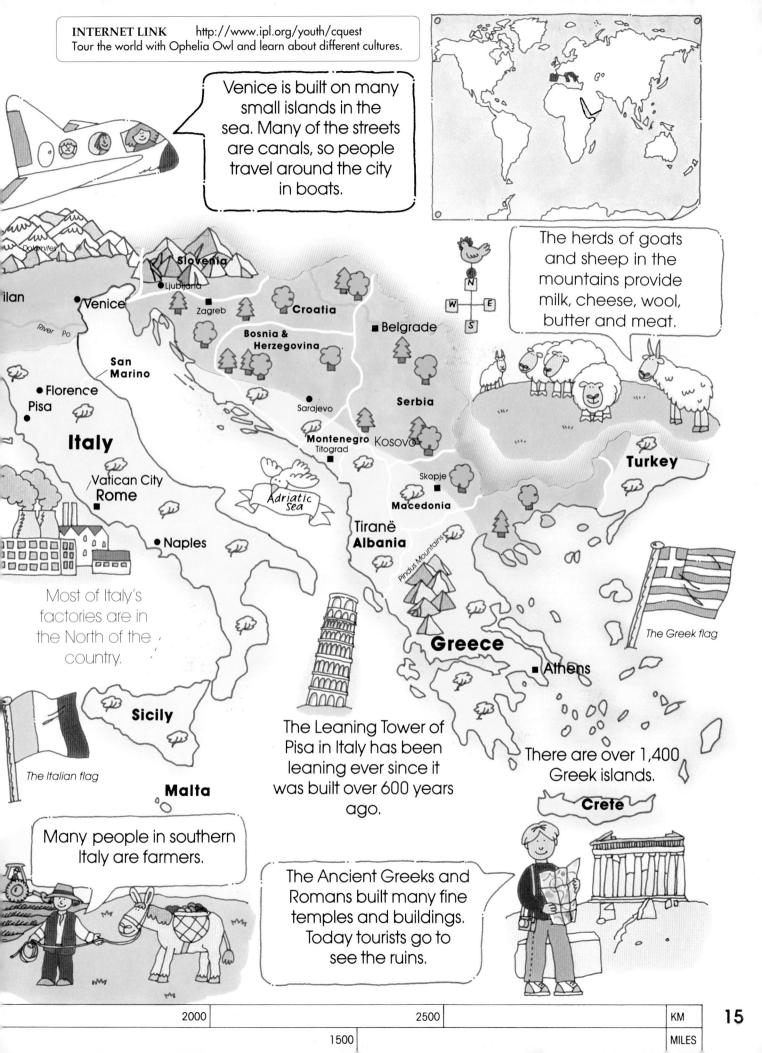

Venice is built on many small islands in the sea. Many of the streets are canals, so people travel around the city in boats.

The herds of goats and sheep in the mountains provide milk, cheese, wool, butter and meat.

Dolomites

Slovenia

Ljubljana

Zagreb

Croatia

ilan

Venice

River Po

Bosnia & Herzegovina

Belgrade

San Marino

Florence

Pisa

Sarajevo

Serbia

Italy

Montenegro
Titograd

Kosovo

Turkey

Vatican City
Rome

Adriatic Sea

Skopje

Macedonia

Naples

Tiranë
Albania

Pindus Mountains

Greece

The Greek flag

Most of Italy's factories are in the North of the country.

Athens

There are over 1,400 Greek islands.

Sicily

The Leaning Tower of Pisa in Italy has been leaning ever since it was built over 600 years ago.

Crete

The Italian flag

Malta

Many people in southern Italy are farmers.

The Ancient Greeks and Romans built many fine temples and buildings. Today tourists go to see the ruins.

| | 2000 | | 2500 | | KM |
| | | 1500 | | | MILES |

Africa

INTERNET LINK   http://www.ks-connection.org
Find a penfriend from another country!

Africa is the second largest continent in the world. It is split up into lots of different countries. Most of Africa is covered in grassland and desert. Some of the tropical rain forests in Africa have been chopped down to build villages and farms.

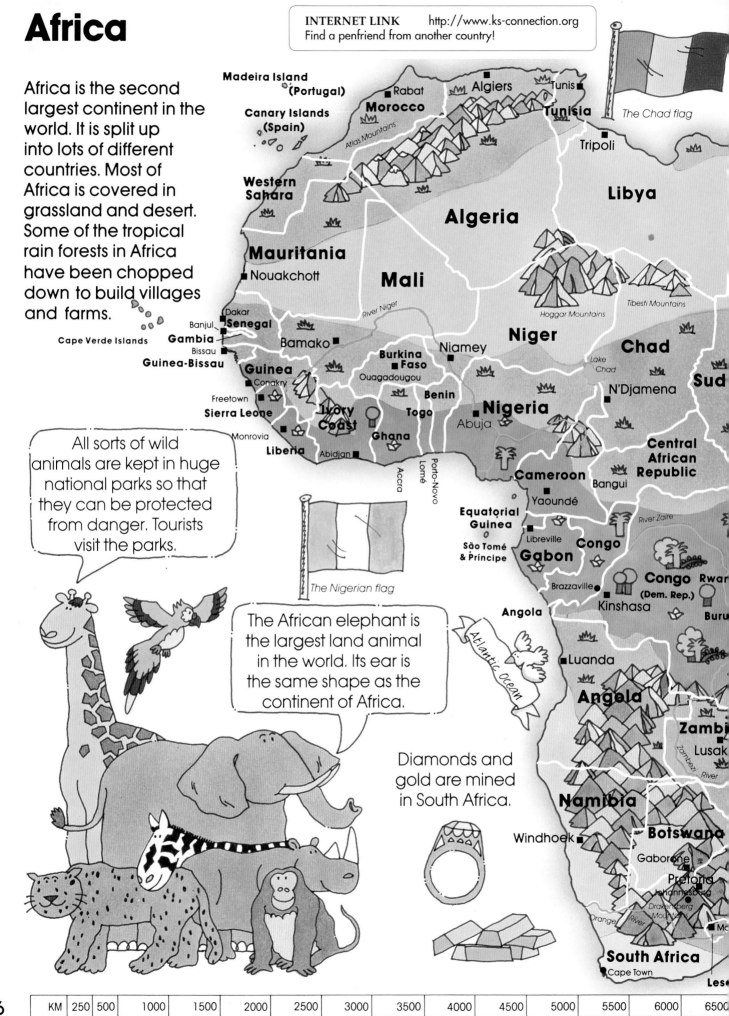

The Chad flag

Madeira Island (Portugal)

Canary Islands (Spain)

Rabat

Algiers

Tunis

Morocco

Tunisia

Tripoli

Atlas Mountains

Libya

Western Sahara

Algeria

Mauritania

Nouakchott

Mali

River Niger

Hoggar Mountains

Tibesti Mountains

Cape Verde Islands

Dakar

Banjul

Senegal

Gambia

Bissau

Guinea-Bissau

Bamako

Niger

Niamey

Lake Chad

Chad

N'Djamena

Sud

Guinea

Conakry

Freetown

Sierra Leone

Monrovia

Liberia

Abidjan

Ivory Coast

Ghana

Accra

Burkina Faso

Ouagadougou

Benin

Togo

Lomé

Porto-Novo

Nigeria

Abuja

Central African Republic

Bangui

Cameroon

Yaoundé

Equatorial Guinea

São Tomé & Príncipe

Libreville

Congo

River Zaire

Gabon

Brazzaville

Congo (Dem. Rep.)

Kinshasa

Rwar

Buru

Angola

Atlantic Ocean

Luanda

Angola

Zambi

Lusak

Zambezi River

The Nigerian flag

Diamonds and gold are mined in South Africa.

Namibia

Windhoek

Botswana

Gaborone

Pretoria

Johannesburg

Drakensberg Mountains

Orange River

South Africa

Cape Town

Lese

All sorts of wild animals are kept in huge national parks so that they can be protected from danger. Tourists visit the parks.

The African elephant is the largest land animal in the world. Its ear is the same shape as the continent of Africa.

KM	250	500	1000	1500	2000	2500	3000	3500	4000	4500	5000	5500	6000	6500
MILES		250	500	1000		1500		2000		2500		3000		3500	4000

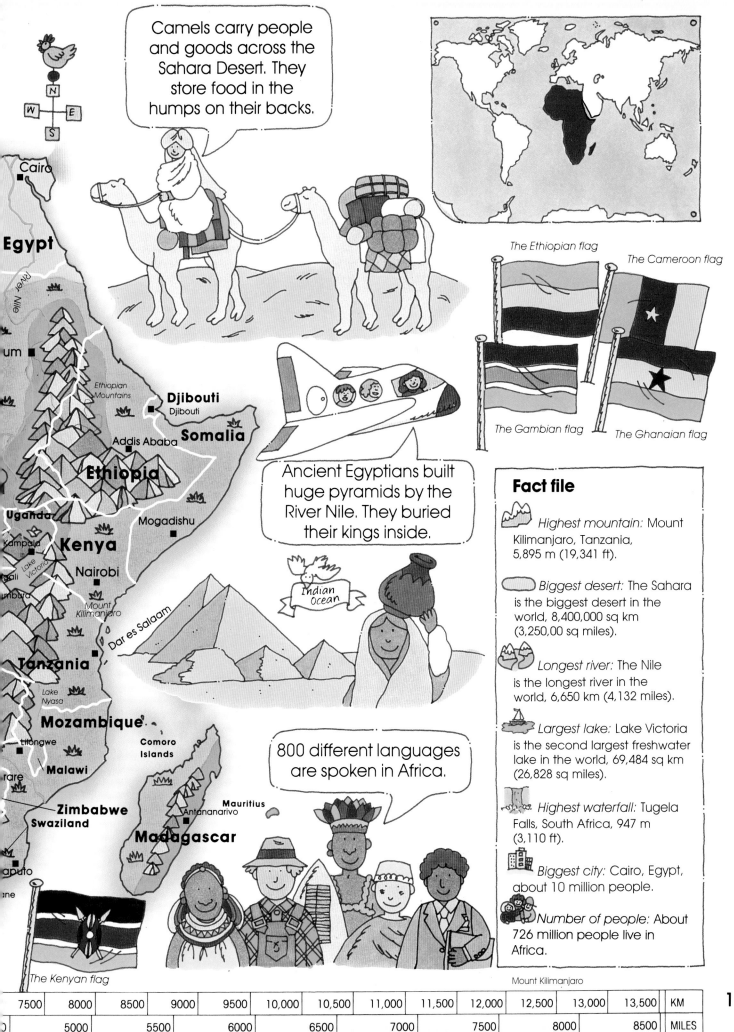

Camels carry people and goods across the Sahara Desert. They store food in the humps on their backs.

The Ethiopian flag

The Cameroon flag

The Gambian flag

The Ghanaian flag

Ancient Egyptians built huge pyramids by the River Nile. They buried their kings inside.

Indian Ocean

800 different languages are spoken in Africa.

The Kenyan flag

Fact file

Highest mountain: Mount Kilimanjaro, Tanzania, 5,895 m (19,341 ft).

Biggest desert: The Sahara is the biggest desert in the world, 8,400,000 sq km (3,250,00 sq miles).

Longest river: The Nile is the longest river in the world, 6,650 km (4,132 miles).

Largest lake: Lake Victoria is the second largest freshwater lake in the world, 69,484 sq km (26,828 sq miles).

Highest waterfall: Tugela Falls, South Africa, 947 m (3,110 ft).

Biggest city: Cairo, Egypt, about 10 million people.

Number of people: About 726 million people live in Africa.

Mount Kilimanjaro

Cairo · Egypt · River Nile · um · Ethiopian Mountains · Djibouti · Djibouti · Somalia · Addis Ababa · Ethiopia · Uganda · Mogadishu · Kampala · Kenya · Lake Victoria · Nairobi · Mount Kilimanjaro · Dar es Salaam · Tanzania · Lake Nyasa · Mozambique · Lilongwe · Comoro Islands · Malawi · Zimbabwe · Swaziland · Mauritius · Antananarivo · Madagascar · aputo

7500	8000	8500	9000	9500	10,000	10,500	11,000	11,500	12,000	12,500	13,000	13,500	KM
	5000		5500		6000		6500		7000		7500		8000	8500	MILES

The Former U.S.S.R.

In 1991 the former U.S.S.R. (the Soviet Union) broke up into 15 separate republics. Estonia, Lithuania and Latvia became fully independent. Most of the other republics agreed to work together in a Commonwealth.

The north is freezing cold, but the deserts in the south are burning hot. In between there are forests and farmlands.

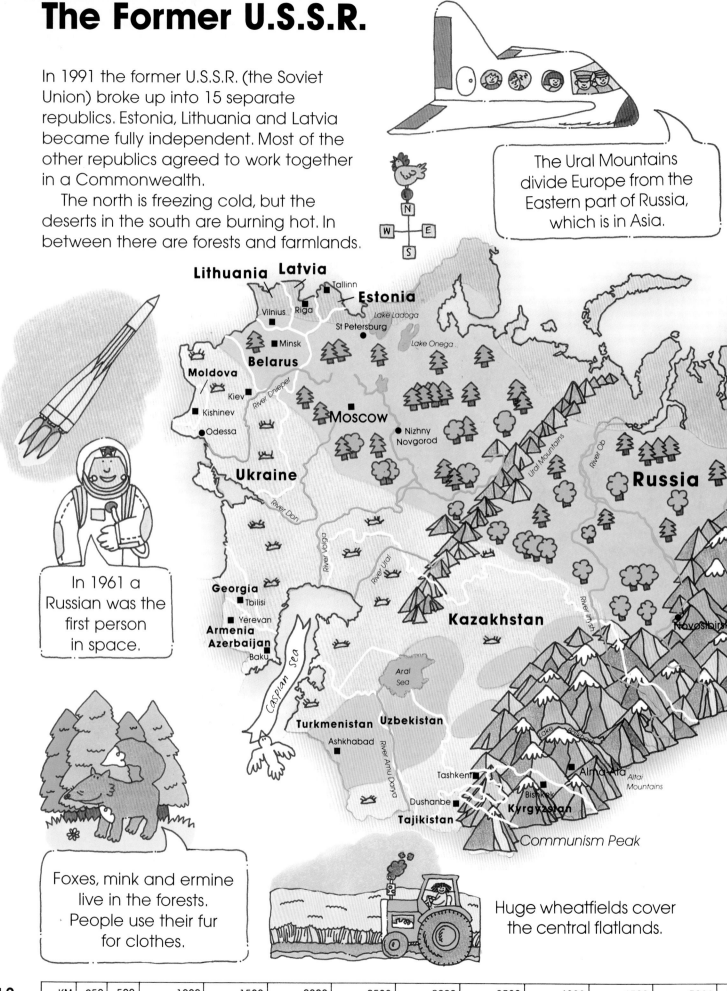

The Ural Mountains divide Europe from the Eastern part of Russia, which is in Asia.

In 1961 a Russian was the first person in space.

Foxes, mink and ermine live in the forests. People use their fur for clothes.

Huge wheatfields cover the central flatlands.

Lithuania
Latvia
Estonia
Tallinn
Vilnius
Riga
Lake Ladoga
St Petersburg
Lake Onega
Belarus
Minsk
Moldova
Kiev
River Dnieper
Kishinev
Odessa
Moscow
Nizhny Novgorod
Ukraine
River Don
River Volga
River Ural
Georgia
Tbilisi
Yerevan
Armenia
Azerbaijan
Baku
Caspian Sea
Aral Sea
Kazakhstan
Ural Mountains
River Ob
Russia
River Irtysh
Novosibirsk
Turkmenistan
Uzbekistan
Ashkhabad
River Amu Darya
Tashkent
Dushanbe
Tajikistan
Bishkek
Kyrgyzstan
Alma-Ata
Altai Mountains
Lake Balkhash
Communism Peak

KM	250	500		1000	1500	2000	2500	3000	3500	4000	4500	5000
MILES		250	500		1000		1500		2000		2500		3000

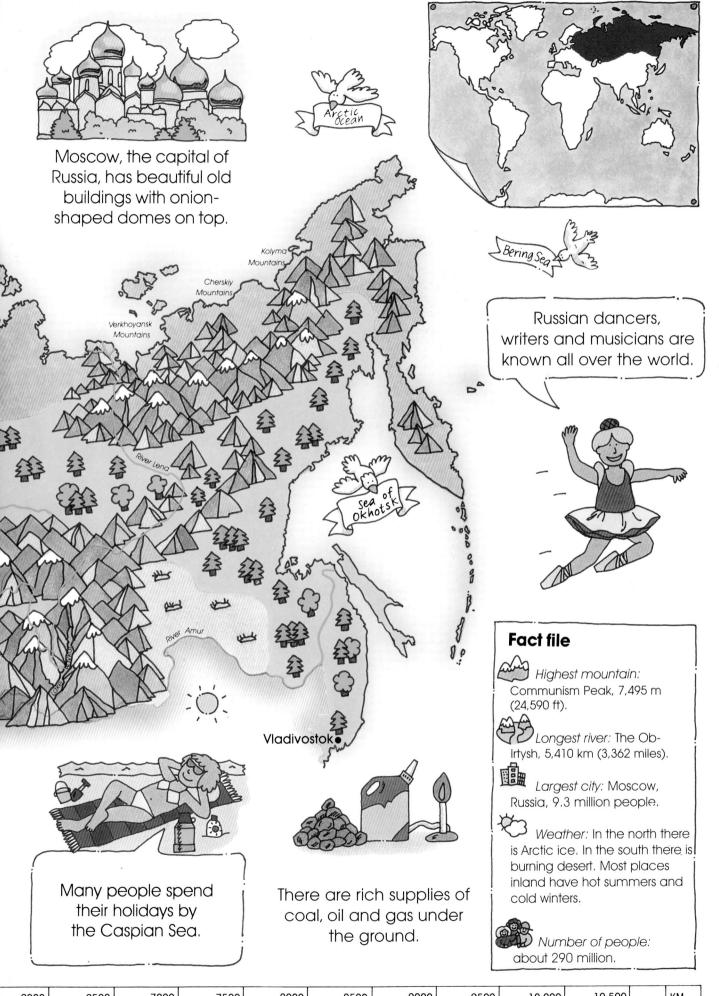

Moscow, the capital of Russia, has beautiful old buildings with onion-shaped domes on top.

Arctic Ocean

Bering Sea

Kolyma Mountains

Cherskiy Mountains

Verkhoyansk Mountains

River Lena

Sea of Okhotsk

River Amur

Vladivostok

Russian dancers, writers and musicians are known all over the world.

Many people spend their holidays by the Caspian Sea.

There are rich supplies of coal, oil and gas under the ground.

Fact file

Highest mountain: Communism Peak, 7,495 m (24,590 ft).

Longest river: The Ob-Irtysh, 5,410 km (3,362 miles).

Largest city: Moscow, Russia, 9.3 million people.

Weather: In the north there is Arctic ice. In the south there is burning desert. Most places inland have hot summers and cold winters.

Number of people: about 290 million.

6000	6500	7000	7500	8000	8500	9000	9500	10,000	10,500	KM
	4000		4500		5000		5500		6000		6500	MILES

The Middle East

INTERNET LINK   http://www.atlapedia.com
Find colourful maps and statistics about the world.

Most of the Middle East is either mountainous or hot, sandy desert. Some of the countries have a great deal of valuable oil under the ground. The oil is pumped up to the surface at oil wells. It is then sold to other countries for use as petrol and other kinds of fuel.

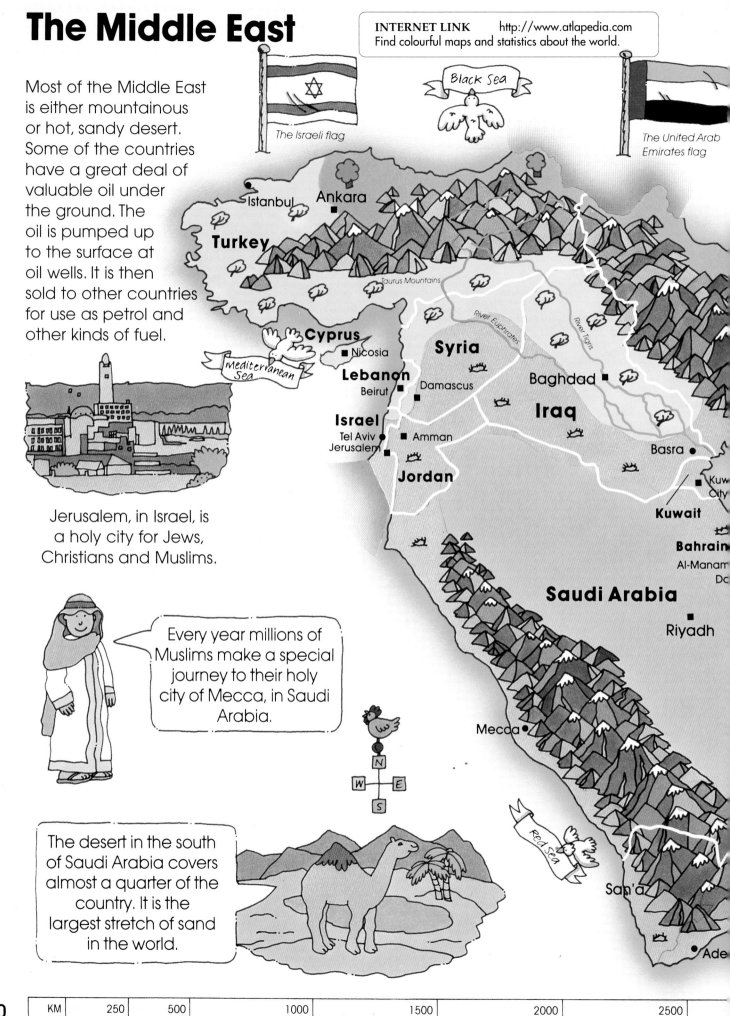

The Israeli flag

The United Arab Emirates flag

Jerusalem, in Israel, is a holy city for Jews, Christians and Muslims.

Every year millions of Muslims make a special journey to their holy city of Mecca, in Saudi Arabia.

The desert in the south of Saudi Arabia covers almost a quarter of the country. It is the largest stretch of sand in the world.

Black Sea

Istanbul
Ankara
Turkey
Taurus Mountains
Cyprus
Nicosia
Mediterranean Sea
Lebanon
Beirut
Syria
Damascus
River Euphrates
River Tigris
Baghdad
Iraq
Israel
Tel Aviv
Jerusalem
Amman
Jordan
Basra
Kuwait
Kuw City
Bahrain
Al-Manam Do
Saudi Arabia
Riyadh
Mecca
Red Sea
San'a
Ade

N
W   E
S

20

KM	250	500	1000	1500	2000	2500
MILES	250	500	1000	1500	

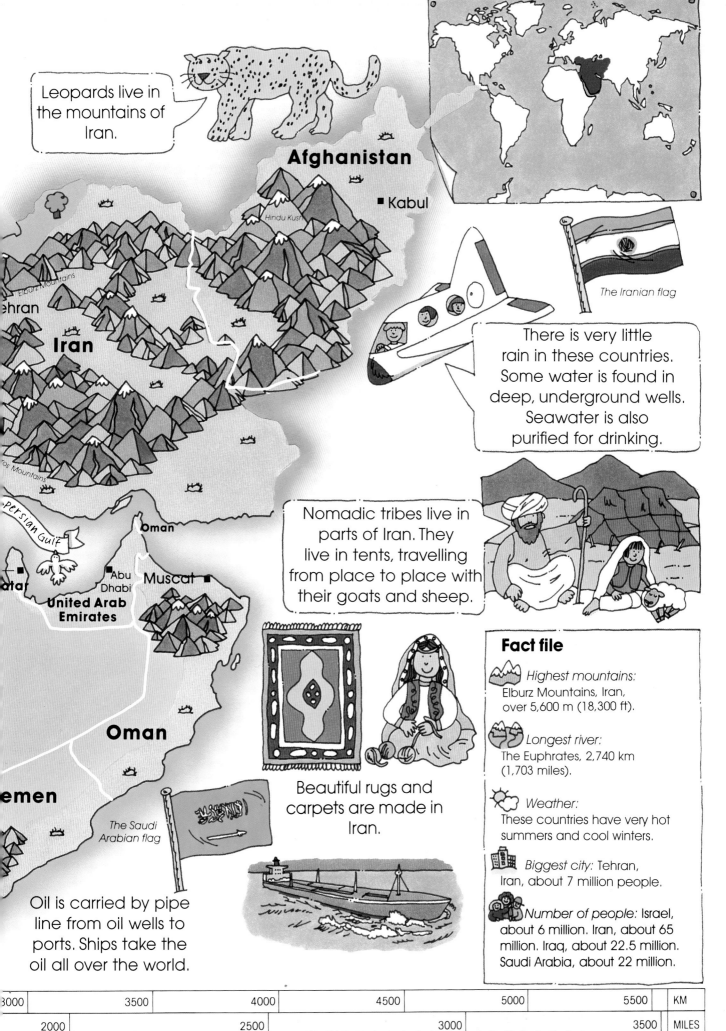

Leopards live in the mountains of Iran.

Afghanistan

■ Kabul

Hindu Kush

Elburz Mountains

ehran

Iran

...ros Mountains

Persian Gulf

Oman

■Abu Dhabi

Muscat ■

...atar

United Arab Emirates

Oman

...emen

The Saudi Arabian flag

The Iranian flag

There is very little rain in these countries. Some water is found in deep, underground wells. Seawater is also purified for drinking.

Nomadic tribes live in parts of Iran. They live in tents, travelling from place to place with their goats and sheep.

Beautiful rugs and carpets are made in Iran.

Oil is carried by pipe line from oil wells to ports. Ships take the oil all over the world.

Fact file

Highest mountains: Elburz Mountains, Iran, over 5,600 m (18,300 ft).

Longest river: The Euphrates, 2,740 km (1,703 miles).

Weather: These countries have very hot summers and cool winters.

Biggest city: Tehran, Iran, about 7 million people.

Number of people: Israel, about 6 million. Iran, about 65 million. Iraq, about 22.5 million. Saudi Arabia, about 22 million.

| 3000 | 3500 | 4000 | 4500 | 5000 | 5500 | KM |
| 2000 | 2500 | 3000 | 3500 | MILES |

South Asia

Much of South Asia is farmland and relies on the heavy monsoon rains between June and October for crops to grow. The Himalayas are the highest mountain range in the world and divide South Asia from China.

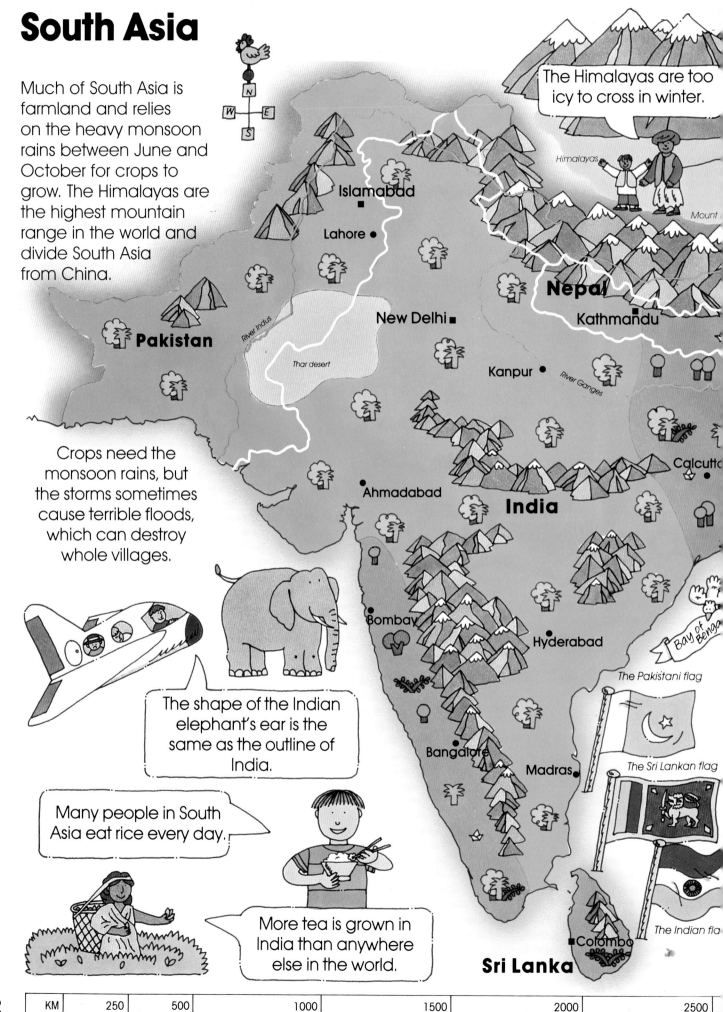

The Himalayas are too icy to cross in winter.

Himalayas

Mount

Nepal

Kathmandu ■

Islamabad ■

Lahore ●

New Delhi ■

River Indus

Thar desert

Kanpur ● *River Ganges*

Pakistan

Calcutta

Crops need the monsoon rains, but the storms sometimes cause terrible floods, which can destroy whole villages.

● Ahmadabad

India

Bombay ●

Hyderabad ●

Bay of Bengal

The Pakistani flag

The shape of the Indian elephant's ear is the same as the outline of India.

Bangalore ●

Madras ●

The Sri Lankan flag

Many people in South Asia eat rice every day.

More tea is grown in India than anywhere else in the world.

■ Colombo

Sri Lanka

The Indian flag

KM	250	500		1000	1500	2000	2500
MILES		250	500		1000		1500

Ponies and yaks are used to carry goods across the Himalayas.

Thimbu
Bhutan
River Brahmaputra
angladesh
Dhaka

Elephants and tigers live on the lower slopes of the Himalayas and in the swamps of the Ganges River.

India is the second most populous country in the world.

Fact file

Highest mountain: Mount Everest, Himalayas, 8,848 m (29,029 ft).

Longest river: Ganges-Brahmaputra, 2,900 km (1,802 miles).

Weather: It is very cold in the mountains, but hot most of the year elsewhere.

Biggest city: Calcutta, India, about 12 million people.

Number of people in some countries:
Nepal, about 24.5 million.
Bangladesh, about 127 million.
Bhutan, about 2 million.
India, about 1 billion.
Sri Lanka, about 19 million.
Pakistan, about 138 million.

Cows are sacred animals in India. They are not kept in fields but are allowed to graze where they like.

Cotton plants produce fibres that are made into cotton fabric. Cotton can be painted or dyed and made into clothes.

The Taj Mahal, near Agra in northern India, is often called the most beautiful building in the world.

3000		3500		4000		4500		5000		KM
	2000			2500			3000			MILES

Southeast Asia

Southeast Asia is an area that curves from Myanmar through a chain of islands towards Australia. It is warm all the year round, but the monsoon wind brings heavy rains. They can damage the traditional houses made of woven palm leaves.

In Thailand, elephants are used to haul trees from the forest to the river. The trees then float down to the sawmills.

The Thai flag

Corals are sea creatures that live in the warm, shallow waters of the Pacific. When they die, their hard skeletons form islands and reefs. Millions of corals are needed to make one small island.

Fishing is a way of life for many islanders. Their boats are like canoes with small sails.

Coral islands when seen from above have a turquoise band of sea around them.

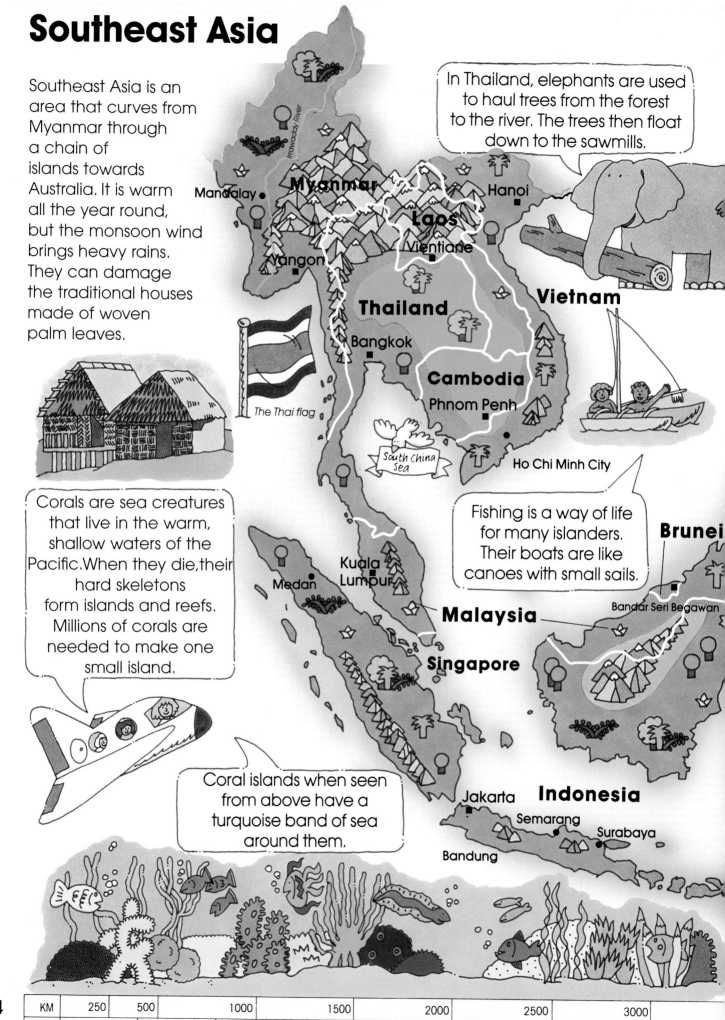

Mandalay

Myanmar

Hanoi

Laos

Vientiane

Yangon

Irrawaddy River

Thailand

Vietnam

Bangkok

Cambodia

Phnom Penh

South China Sea

Ho Chi Minh City

Brunei

Kuala Lumpur

Medan

Bandar Seri Begawan

Malaysia

Singapore

Jakarta

Indonesia

Semarang

Surabaya

Bandung

KM	250	500	1000	1500	2000	2500	3000
MILES	250	500	1000	1500	2000

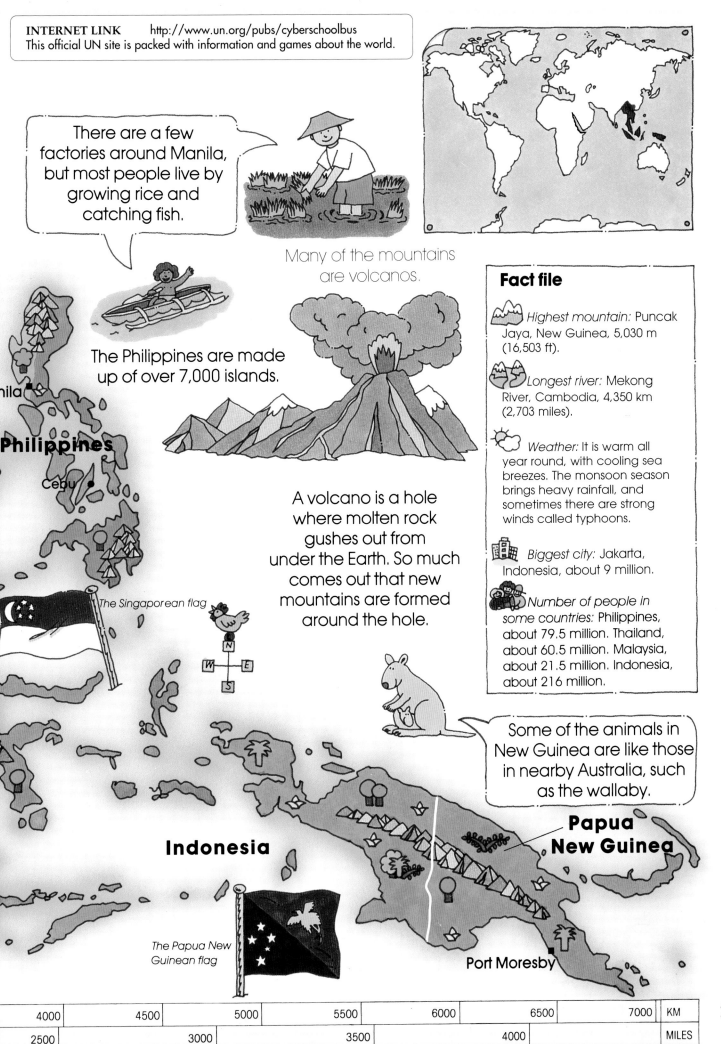

There are a few factories around Manila, but most people live by growing rice and catching fish.

Many of the mountains are volcanos.

The Philippines are made up of over 7,000 islands.

Philippines

Cebu

The Singaporean flag

A volcano is a hole where molten rock gushes out from under the Earth. So much comes out that new mountains are formed around the hole.

Fact file

Highest mountain: Puncak Jaya, New Guinea, 5,030 m (16,503 ft).

Longest river: Mekong River, Cambodia, 4,350 km (2,703 miles).

Weather: It is warm all year round, with cooling sea breezes. The monsoon season brings heavy rainfall, and sometimes there are strong winds called typhoons.

Biggest city: Jakarta, Indonesia, about 9 million.

Number of people in some countries: Philippines, about 79.5 million. Thailand, about 60.5 million. Malaysia, about 21.5 million. Indonesia, about 216 million.

Some of the animals in New Guinea are like those in nearby Australia, such as the wallaby.

Papua New Guinea

Indonesia

The Papua New Guinean flag

Port Moresby

4000	4500	5000	5500	6000	6500	7000	KM
2500		3000		3500		4000		MILES

East Asia

INTERNET LINK   http://www.mrdowling.com
This is a kids' geography and history site, packed with fascinating facts.

China is the third largest country in the world. Japan is much smaller, about the same size as Britain, but it is the richest country in Asia.

Chinese temples and pagodas have tiled roofs that curl up at the corners.

The Mongolian flag

Ulan Bator

Altai Mountains

Mongolia

Gobi Desert

China

Huang He

Taiyuo

Tibetan Plateau

Himalayas

Tibet

River Mekang

Xian

Chengdu

Chang Jiang

Fact file

Highest mountain: Mount Everest, 8,848 m (29,029 ft).

Longest river: Chang Jiang, China, 6,418 km (3,988 miles).

Weather: Northern China and Japan have wet summers and dry winters. The south is very hot all year round.

Biggest city: Tokyo, Japan, about 27 million people.

Number of people: Japan, about 126 million. China, about 1.25 billion.

Guangz

The Chinese flag

KM	250	500		1000	1500		2000		2500		3000
MILES		250	500			1000			1500			

Japan has many factories where people make cars, computers and televisions.

The Japanese flag

River Amur

Harbin

Sea of Japan

Hokkaido

Shen-yang

North Korea

The ancient kingdom of Korea was divided into North and South Korea after the Second World War.

Pyongyang

Seoul

South Korea

Hiroshima

Kyoto

Tokyo

Japan

The Great Wall of China was built over 2,000 years ago to keep out enemies. It winds 2,414 km (1,500 miles) across the hills of northern China.

Yellow Sea

Nagasaki

Pacific Ocean

Rice is grown in paddy fields. These are fields that are flooded by the rains or by rivers.

...ing

...anjing

Shanghai

The South Korean flag

Taipei

Taiwan

Hong Kong

The North Korean flag

A fifth of the world's population lives in China.

Bears and a few giant pandas live in the southwest of China.

| 3500 | 4000 | 4500 | 5000 | 5500 | 6000 | KM |
| | 2500 | | 3000 | | 3500 | MILES |

Australia and New Zealand

Australia is the smallest continent in the world. It lies in the southern Pacific Ocean, on the opposite side of the world from Europe. New Zealand is 1,500 km (900 miles) southeast of Australia. Most of Australia is flat and dry. New Zealand is more hilly and green.

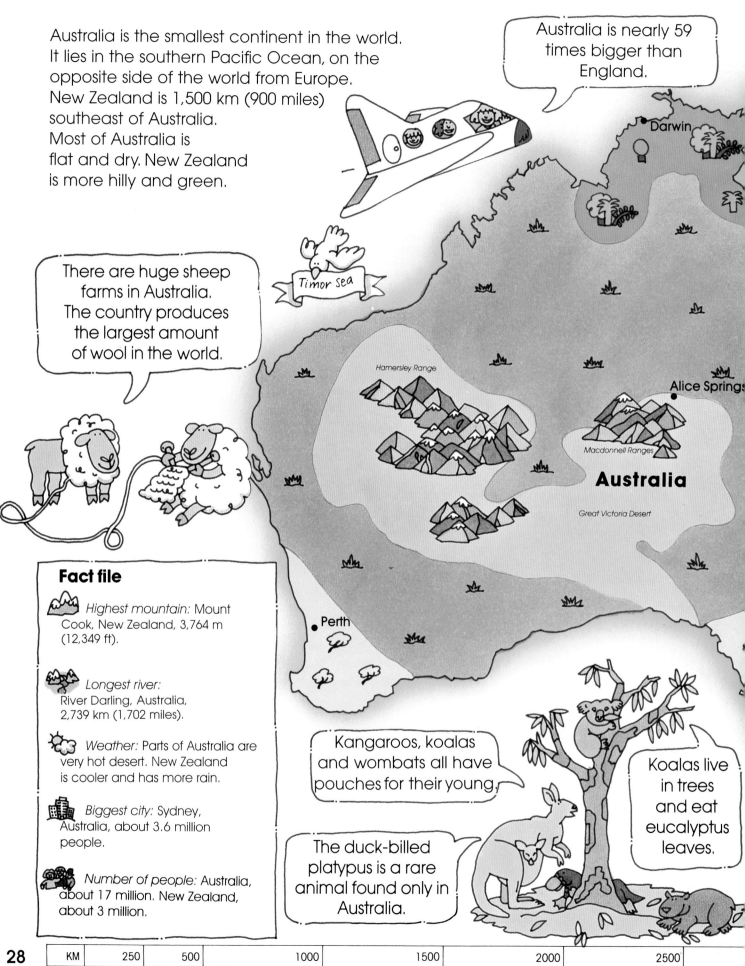

Australia is nearly 59 times bigger than England.

There are huge sheep farms in Australia. The country produces the largest amount of wool in the world.

Timor Sea

Darwin

Hamersley Range

Alice Springs

Macdonnell Ranges

Australia

Great Victoria Desert

Perth

Fact file

Highest mountain: Mount Cook, New Zealand, 3,764 m (12,349 ft).

Longest river: River Darling, Australia, 2,739 km (1,702 miles).

Weather: Parts of Australia are very hot desert. New Zealand is cooler and has more rain.

Biggest city: Sydney, Australia, about 3.6 million people.

Number of people: Australia, about 17 million. New Zealand, about 3 million.

Kangaroos, koalas and wombats all have pouches for their young.

Koalas live in trees and eat eucalyptus leaves.

The duck-billed platypus is a rare animal found only in Australia.

KM		250		500		1000		1500		2000		2500
MILES			250		500			1000			1500	

The Great Barrier Reef is the biggest coral reef in the world.

Many plants and fish live on and around coral reefs.

Surfing is a popular sport in Australia.

The Aborigines were the first people to settle in Australia. They used to hunt and fight with boomerangs.

Cairns

The Great Barrier Reef

Great Dividing Range

Brisbane

River Darling

River Murray

Adelaide

Sydney

Canberra

Melbourne

Tasman Sea

Hobart **Tasmania**

The Australian flag

New Zealand

New Zealand has two islands called North Island and South Island.

NORTH ISLAND

Auckland

The kiwi is one of the national emblems of New Zealand. It cannot fly.
Mount Cook

Wellington

Christchurch

The New Zealand flag

SOUTH ISLAND

	3500		4000		KM
2000			2500		MILES

KM	250		500		1000	KM
MILES		250		500		MILES

The Arctic

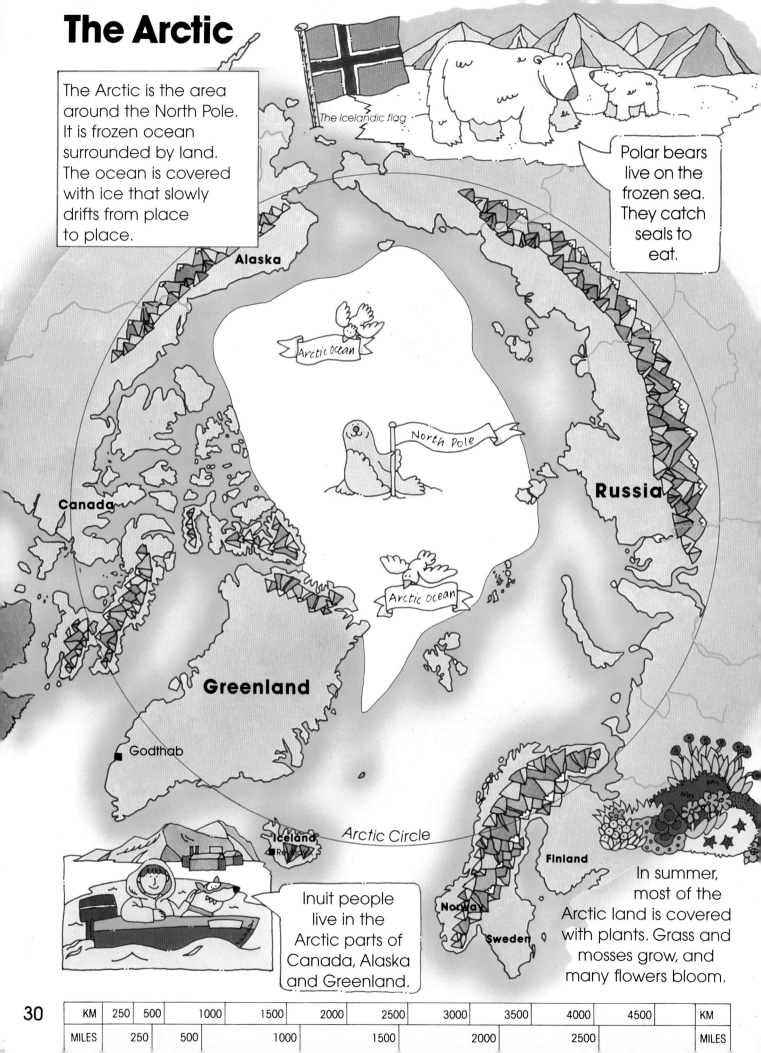

The Arctic is the area around the North Pole. It is frozen ocean surrounded by land. The ocean is covered with ice that slowly drifts from place to place.

The Icelandic flag

Polar bears live on the frozen sea. They catch seals to eat.

Alaska

Arctic Ocean

North Pole

Arctic Ocean

Canada

Russia

Greenland

Godthab

Arctic Circle

Iceland

Reykjavik

Finland

Norway

Sweden

Inuit people live in the Arctic parts of Canada, Alaska and Greenland.

In summer, most of the Arctic land is covered with plants. Grass and mosses grow, and many flowers bloom.

KM	250	500	1000	1500	2000	2500	3000	3500	4000	4500	KM
MILES		250	500	1000		1500	2000		2500		MILES

The Antarctic

The Antarctic is ice-covered land around the South Pole. The ice is 4,500 metres (14,800 feet) thick in some places. There are many high mountains and some volancos.

At the North and South Poles, winter and summer last six months each. Winter is dark all day and night. In summer it is light all the time.

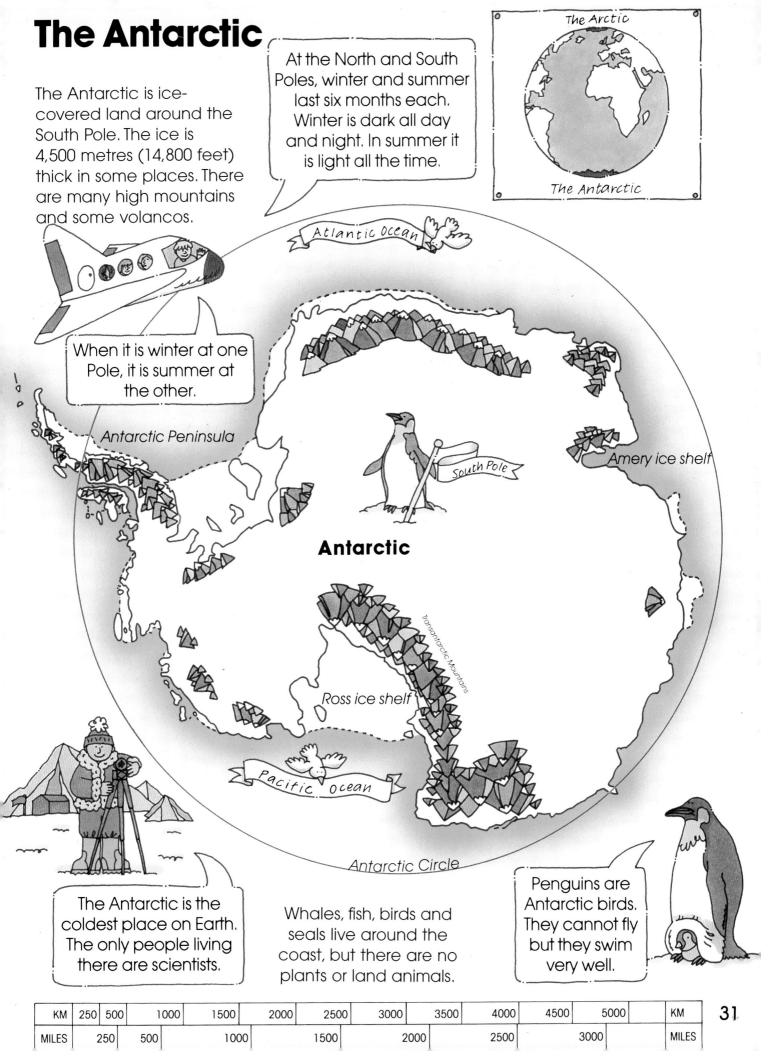

The Arctic

The Antarctic

Atlantic Ocean

When it is winter at one Pole, it is summer at the other.

Antarctic Peninsula

Amery ice shelf

South Pole

Antarctic

Transantarctic Mountains

Ross ice shelf

Pacific Ocean

Antarctic Circle

The Antarctic is the coldest place on Earth. The only people living there are scientists.

Whales, fish, birds and seals live around the coast, but there are no plants or land animals.

Penguins are Antarctic birds. They cannot fly but they swim very well.

KM	250	500	1000	1500	2000	2500	3000	3500	4000	4500	5000	KM
MILES		250	500	1000		1500	2000		2500		3000	MILES

Index

INTERNET LINK   http://www.bbc.co.uk/education/landmarks/high/menu.html
Tour the world, habitat by habitat. Discover the environmental problems facing the planet.

© 2002 Zigzag Children's Books,
an imprint of Chrysalis Children's Books,
64 Brewery Road, London, N7 9NT

Every effort has been made to ensure none of the
recommended websites in this book is linked to
inappropriate material. However, due to the
ever-changing nature of the Internet, the publishers
regret they cannot take responsibility for future
content of these websites.

British Library Cataloguing in Publication Data for this
book is available from the British Library.

ISBN 1 903954 46 0 (hb) ISBN 1 903954 50 9 (pb)

Printed and bound in China

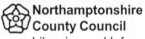